BOOK 1 • Cornet/Trumpet

COMPREHENSIVE BAND METHOD

MW01153172

BEST IN CLASS

Dear Student,

Welcome to BEST IN CLASS!

Music is an important part of our daily lives. The study of music helps us gain an appreciation for beauty and a feeling of sensitivity. It also provides an avenue for creativity and recognition, as well as a demand for self-discipline. All of these are important in our world today.

Playing a musical instrument can also give you years of enjoyment. To play your instrument well, careful practice is essential. You will find a chart below to help you keep track of your practice time. Always strive to do your best.

Best wishes in reaching your musical goals!

Bruce Pearson

PRACTICE RECORD CHART

WEEK	DAY 1	DAY 2	DAY 3	DAY 4	DAY 5	DAY 6	DAY 7	TOTAL TIME	PARENT'S INITIALS	WEEKLY GRADE
1										
2										
3										
4										
5										
6										
7										
8										
9										
10										
11										
12										
13										
14										
15										
16										
17										
18										

WEEK	DAY 1	DAY 2	DAY 3	DAY 4	DAY 5	DAY 6	DAY 7	TOTAL TIME	PARENT'S INITIALS	WEEKLY GRADE
19										
20										
21										
22										
23										
24										
25										
26										
27										
28										
29										
30										
31										
32										
33										
34										
35										
36										

© 1982 Kjos West, Publisher, San Diego, California
ISBN 0-8497-5842-4   All Rights Reserved   International Copyright Secured   Printed in U.S.A.   W3TP

BEFORE YOU START . . .

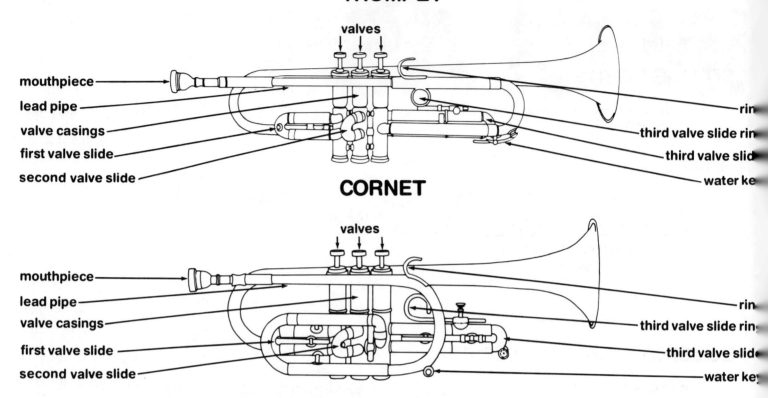

TRUMPET

valves

mouthpiece
lead pipe
valve casings
first valve slide
second valve slide

rin
third valve slide rin
third valve slid
water ke

CORNET

valves

mouthpiece
lead pipe
valve casings
first valve slide
second valve slide

rin
third valve slide rin
third valve slid
water key

ASSEMBLING YOUR INSTRUMENT

- Hold your instrument in your LEFT hand.
- Hold the **mouthpiece** with your RIGHT hand and place it into the **lead pipe.**
- Gently turn the mouthpiece to the right (NOT TOO TIGHT).

HOLDING YOUR INSTRUMENT

- Place your LEFT hand around the **valve casings.** Hold your instrument firmly but without tension. If your instrument has a **ring** on the **third valve slide,** place your third finger in the ring.
- Place your RIGHT hand as follows:
  1) Place your thumb between the first and second valve casings under the lead pipe.
  2) Place the fleshy part of your first three fingertips on the **valve** tops. These fingers should be slightly curved. In this position your right hand should form a backward "C."
  3) Place your little finger ON the **ring** (not IN the ring).
- Keep both wrists straight.

GETTING A GOOD TONE . . .

POSITIONING YOUR MOUTHPIECE

- Position your mouthpiece on your lips so that it is centered, with approximately one-half of your upper lip and one-half of yrour lower lip within the mouthpiece rim. ·
- Ask your director if your mouthpiece placement is acceptable.

FORMING THE EMBOUCHURE

- Bring your lips lightly together as if saying the letter "m."
- Holding your lips together, slightly separate your upper and lower teeth.
- It is important to have firm corners but a relaxed center of your lips.
- Remember . . . the embouchure is formed into place, NOT blown into place.
- The embouchure must be formed without tension. NEVER use a smile to form an embouchure.
- Ask your director to check your embouchure.
- Check your embouchure regularly in front of a mirror.

SITTING POSITION

- Sit on the edge of your chair, spine straight, shoulders back, and both feet flat on the floor.

WIND SPEED

- Take a full breath by inhaling through the corners of your mouth.
- Be sure NOT to raise your shoulders while inhaling.
- GOOD WIND SPEED IS ESSENTIAL TO:
  1) Good tone quality
  2) Endurance
  3) Range
  4) Intonation
  5) Good tonguing

BUZZING YOUR MOUTHPIECE

- Hold your mouthpiece at the far end of the mouthpiece shank with your thumb and first finger.
- Form your embouchure as already described.
- Position your mouthpiece as already described.
- Take a full breath of air and blow, creating a nice, "free" buzzing tone.

STARTING EXERCISES

- **"Buzz Saw Blues"**
  Buzz on your mouthpiece for 4 beats, rest for 4 beats. Repeat this 4 times.
- **"The Fireman's Siren"**
  With your mouthpiece only, buzz a starting tone. Then create a siren effect by going up or down and back to your starting tone. To create the higher tones, gradually make the opening in your lips smaller. To go back to the starting tone, gradually relax your lips and make the opening larger.

CARING FOR YOUR INSTRUMENT . . .

- When pulling any of the valve slides, always depress the corresponding valve.
- To oil the valves, follow these steps:
  1) Depress the first valve and pull out the slide that leads to that valve.
  2) Place 5 or 6 drops of valve oil into one of the tubes leading to that valve.
  3) Replace the slide. Remember to hold the valve down.
  4) Rapidly move all of the valves up and down. The oil will "work" its way around all three valves.
- Be sure to grease the slides regularly. Ask your director ro recommend a grease to be used and how it should be applied.
- Use the **water key** to empty the water from your instrument.
- Wipe off your instrument with a soft clean cloth after playing. Then return your instrument to its case.

GETTING A HEAD START...

THE BASICS

VALVES	STAFF	TREBLE CLEF
o = valve up ● = valve down	ledger line	F D B G E / lines — E C A F / space

THE "NATURAL" WAY TO START

SITTING	HOLDING YOUR INSTRUMENT	PLAYING YOUR INSTRUMENT
Be sure you are sitting on the edge of your chair, spine straight, shoulders back, both feet flat on the floor.	Check again for the correct way to hold your instrument (see page 2).	Check again for the correct way to produce a tone on your instrument (see page 2).

IF YOUR "NATURAL" NOTE IS G, PLAY THIS PAGE.

A. THE 1ST NOTE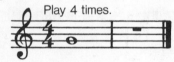

B. THE 2ND NOTE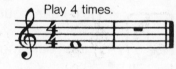

C. TWO'S COMPANY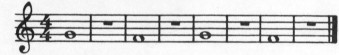

D. A LITTLE EXTRA PRACTICE

E. THE 3RD NOTE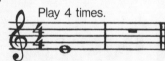

F. THREE TO GET READY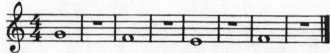

G. THE 4TH NOTE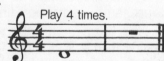

H. THE 5TH NOTE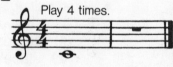

I. PUTTING IT TOGETHER

J. FIVE MAKES A TEAM

for cornets/trumpets only

MEASURES	TIME SIGNATURE	WHOLE NOTE	WHOLE REST
bar lines / measures	4/4 = 4 beats in each measure	o = 4 beats	= 4 beats of silence

WHAT DO YOU HEAR?

When you play your instrument, you will probably play one of these two notes:

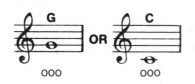

WHAT NEXT?

Ask your director which note you are playing.
If your natural note is G, start on page 4.
If your natural note is C, start on page 5.

IF YOUR "NATURAL" NOTE IS C, PLAY THIS PAGE.

A. THE 1ST NOTE

NEW NOTE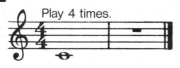

B. THE 2ND NOTE
NEW NOTE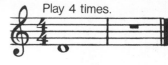

C. TWO'S COMPANY

D. A LITTLE EXTRA PRACTICE

E. THE 3RD NOTE
NEW NOTE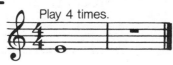

F. THREE TO GET READY
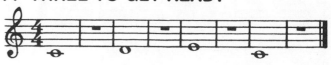

G. THE 4TH NOTE
NEW NOTE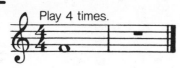

H. THE 5TH NOTE
NEW NOTE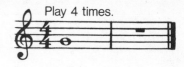

I. PUTTING IT TOGETHER
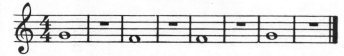

J. FIVE MAKES A TEAM
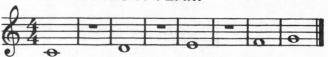

W3TP

6

STARTING TOGETHER...

THE BASICS

VALVES	STAFF	TREBLE CLEF
o = valve up ● = valve down	ledger line	lines spaces

NEW NOTE

1. THE 1ST NOTE

ooo
Play 4 times.
★ Remember the importance of air!

NEW NOTE

2. THE 2ND NOTE

●oo
Play 4 times.

3. WHAT A PAIR!

_____

★ Write in the counting on the blank lines. (Your director will tell you the counting system to use.)

4. HOW DO YOU SOUND?

⌞Band⌟ ⌞Brass⌟ ⌞Band⌟ ⌞Woodwinds⌟ ⌞Band⌟ ⌞Percussion⌟ ⌞Band⌟

★ Which section can play with the best tone quality?

NEW NOTE

5. THE 3RD NOTE

●●o
Play 4 times.
★ Don't "puff out" your cheeks!

6. TWO'S COMPANY
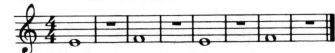

7. THREE TO GET READY
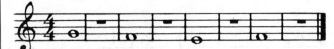

★ Are you playing with a good hand position and a full air stream?

8. A LITTLE EXTRA PRACTICE

THEORY GAME

9. NAME GAME

1. Write the names of the lines in the squares.

2. Write the names of the spaces in the circles.

W3TP

for the full band

MEASURES	TIME SIGNATURE	WHOLE NOTE	WHOLE REST
bar lines / measures	$\frac{4}{4}$ = 4 beats in each measure	𝅝 = 4 beats	= 4 beats of silence

 NEW IDEA

BREATH MARK	,	Take a breath.

10. TWO AT A TIME
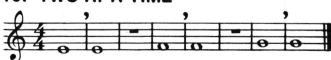

 NEW NOTE

11. THE 4TH NOTE

12. THERE'S ALWAYS ROOM FOR MORE
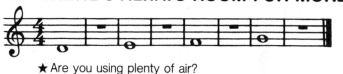

★ Are you using plenty of air?

 NEW NOTE

13. THE 5TH NOTE

14. TWO-TIMERS

15. FIVE MAKES A TEAM

★ Write in the note names before you play.

 NEW IDEAS

QUARTER NOTE	♩ = 1 beat	$\frac{4}{4}$
QUARTER REST	𝄽 = 1 beat of silence	

16. FOUR IN A ROW
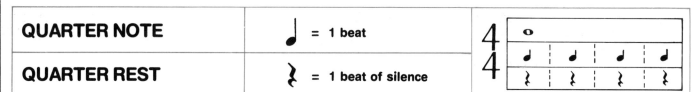

★ Write in the counting before you play.

17. MOVING DOWN

W3TP

NEW IDEA

FERMATA (sometimes called a "hold")	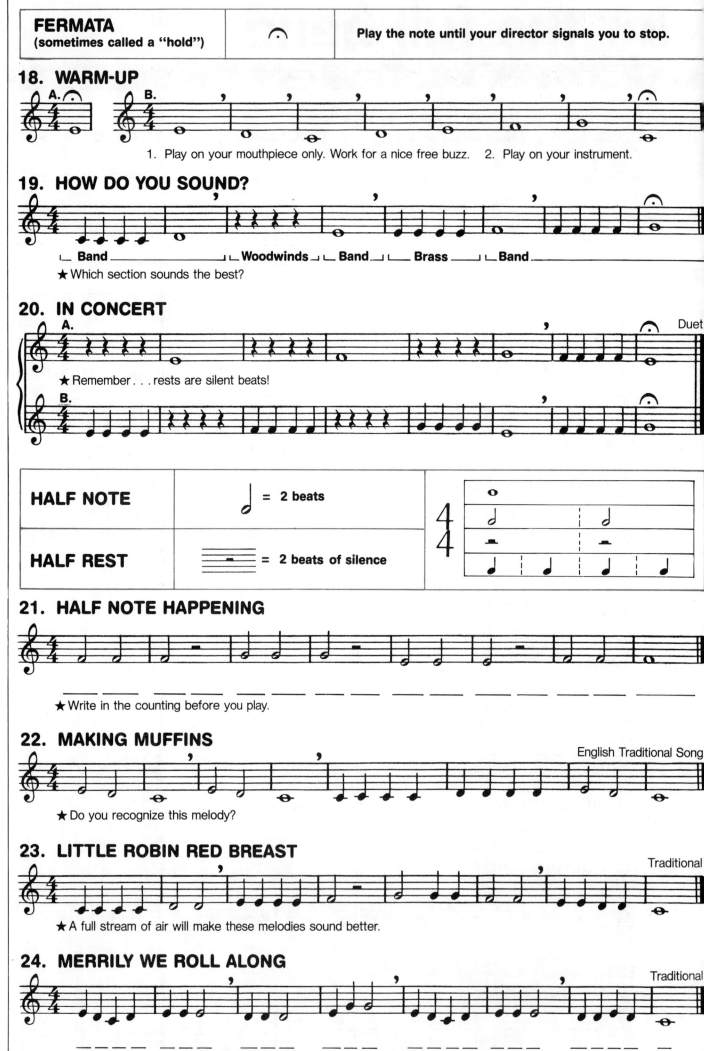	Play the note until your director signals you to stop.

18. WARM-UP

1. Play on your mouthpiece only. Work for a nice free buzz.   2. Play on your instrument.

19. HOW DO YOU SOUND?

└ Band ──────────┘ └ Woodwinds ┘ └ Band ┘ └ Brass ──────┘ └ Band ──────┘

★ Which section sounds the best?

20. IN CONCERT

Duet

★ Remember . . . rests are silent beats!

HALF NOTE	♩ = 2 beats
HALF REST	▬ = 2 beats of silence

21. HALF NOTE HAPPENING

★ Write in the counting before you play.

22. MAKING MUFFINS

English Traditional Song

★ Do you recognize this melody?

23. LITTLE ROBIN RED BREAST

Traditional

★ A full stream of air will make these melodies sound better.

24. MERRILY WE ROLL ALONG

Traditional

★ Write in the note names before you play.

NEW IDEAS

25. WARM-UP

1. Play on your mouthpiece only. Make it smooth and even.   2. Play on your instrument.

| REPEAT SIGN | | Play the previous section of music again. |

26. PLAYING MORE HALF NOTES AND RESTS

27. O COME, LITTLE CHILDREN

J.A.P. Schultz

★ Write in the counting before you play.

28. START TODAY

Traditional

29. FOLLOW THAT MAN

Root - Duet

30. FRENCH SONG

French Folk Song

31. SPELLING GAME

P R __ __ T I __ __   M __ K __ S   P __ R __ __ __ T!

★ Write in the note names.

SOMETHING SPECIAL . . . for cornets/trumpets only

★ Keep the air moving.

W3TP

32. WARM-UP

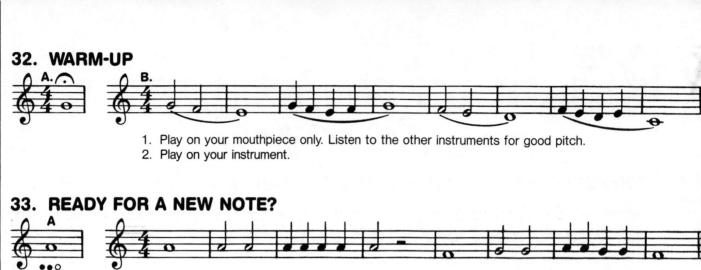

1. Play on your mouthpiece only. Listen to the other instruments for good pitch.
2. Play on your instrument.

NEW NOTE

33. READY FOR A NEW NOTE?

34. IN HARMONY

Duet

35. LIP AND TECHNIC BUILDER

★ Write in the counting before you play.

36. TOM DOOLEY AND HIS FRIEND

Folk Song - Duet

37. ODE TO JOY

Ludwig van Beethoven

★ Are you playing with a good hand position?

SOMETHING SPECIAL...for cornets/trumpets only

SPECIAL
EXERCISE

★ Are you getting a big tone?

W3TP

EIGHTH NOTE

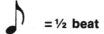 = ½ beat

An eighth note is half as long as a quarter note.

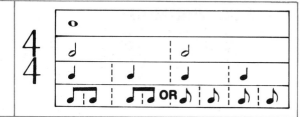

38. EIGHTH NOTE COUNTING AND PLAYING

1. Count the rhythm.   2. Write in the counting before you play.

39. CALYPSO SONG

40. CHA CHA RHYTHM

★Write in the counting before you play.

41. YANKEE DOODLE CHA CHA

42. FEEL THE PULSE

★Write in the counting before you play.

43. SQUARE DANCE

44. MOVIN' ON UP

★Write in the counting before you play.

45. THE TALENT SHOW

46. UNEXPECTED EIGHTHS

W3TP

47. WARM-UP

1. Play on your mouthpiece only. Work for a nice free buzz.   2. Play on your instrument.

48. TECHNIC BUILDER

NEW NOTE

49. AURA LEE

G.R. Poulton

50. OLD MAC'S FARMYARD

NEW IDEA

DOTTED HALF NOTE

2 + 1 = 3 beats
**A dot after a note adds
half the value of the note.**

51. THE DOT MAKES A DIFFERENCE

★ Write in the counting before you play.

THEORY GAME

52. HELPING HAYDN

Franz Joseph Haydn

★ Draw in the bar lines before you play.

NEW IDEA

**TUTTI
SOLO/SOLI**

Tutti = everyone plays
Solo = only one person plays / Soli = only one section plays

53. PAW PAW PATCH

Tutti   Solo/Soli   Tutti   American Singing Game

Tutti   Solo/Soli   Tutti

★ Are you playing with a good hand position?

NEW IDEA

| TIME SIGNATURE | $\frac{3}{4}$ = 3 beats in each measure | 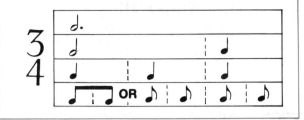 |

54. HEY, DIDDLE DIDDLE
Traditional

55. BLOW THE MAN DOWN
Traditional Sea Chantey

★ Write in the counting before you play.

NEW IDEA

| TIE | | A tie is a curved line that connects two notes of the *same* pitch. Hold the note for the combined value of the two notes. |

56. THE TOTAL IS WHAT COUNTS

57. AUTUMN LEAVES ARE FALLING
German Folk Song - Duet

58. LOVELY EVENING
3-Part Round

SOMETHING SPECIAL...for cornets/trumpets only

SPECIAL EXERCISE

★ How's your wind speed?

59. RHYTHM PUZZLE

THEORY GAME

1. Draw in the bar lines. 2. Clap the rhythm before you play.

60. WARM-UP

1. Play on your mouthpiece only.   2. Play on your instrument.

FLAT	♭		A flat lowers a note ½ step. It remains in effect for the entire measure.

61. TONE DEVELOPER

KEY SIGNATURE		Key signatures change certain notes throughout a piece of music. When you see this key signature, play all B's as B flats.

62. LITTLE CABIN IN THE WOOD

Traditional

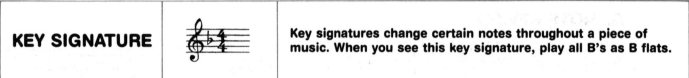

★ Did you check the key signature?

63. THE MAN ON THE FLYING TRAPEZE

George Leybourne

SLUR		A slur is a curved line that connects two notes of *different* pitches. Tongue the first note and move to the second note without tonguing. Keep the air moving.

64. SMOOTH SOUND

65. SLIPPERY SLURS

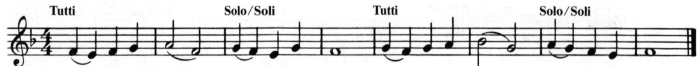

66. SPECIAL EFFECTS

1. Circle the notes changed by the key signature.
2. Write a **T** under all the **ties** and an **S** under all the **slurs** before you play.

W3TP

SOMETHING SPECIAL...for cornets/trumpets only

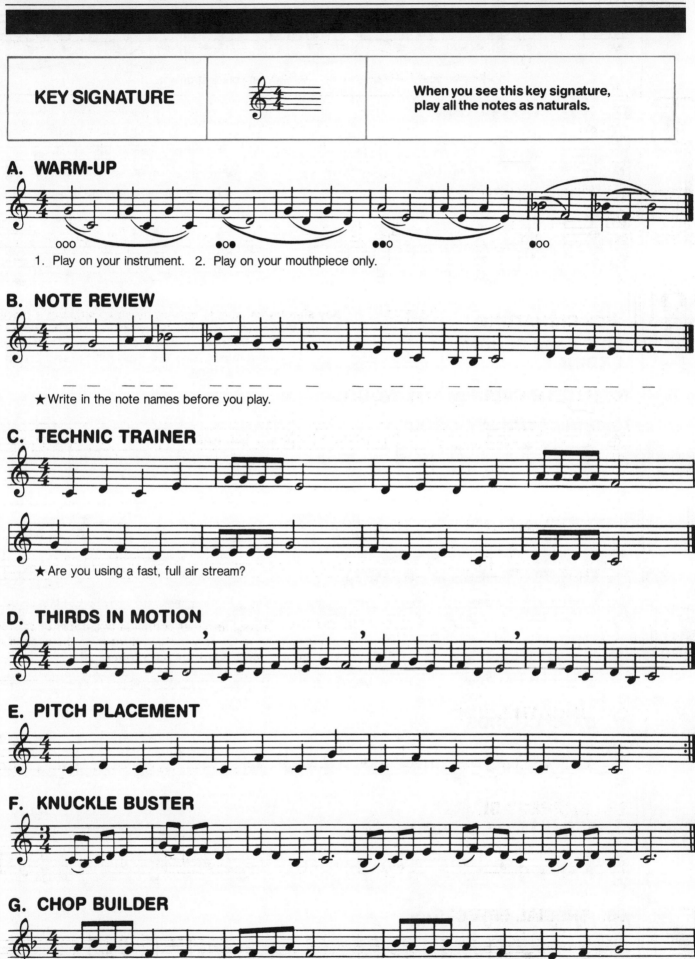

SPECIAL
XERCISES

NEW IDEA

KEY SIGNATURE		When you see this key signature, play all the notes as naturals.

A. WARM-UP

1. Play on your instrument.   2. Play on your mouthpiece only.

B. NOTE REVIEW

★ Write in the note names before you play.

C. TECHNIC TRAINER

★ Are you using a fast, full air stream?

D. THIRDS IN MOTION

E. PITCH PLACEMENT

F. KNUCKLE BUSTER

G. CHOP BUILDER

W3TP

16

67. WARM-UP

1. Play on your mouthpiece only.   2. Play on your instrument.

NEW NOTE

68. HOT CROSS BUNS

English Traditional Song

★ Remember, all B's in this measure are B flats.

69. COPY CATS

★ Is this a B flat or a B natural?

NEW IDEA

| FIRST and SECOND ENDINGS | | Play the first ending the first time. Then repeat the same music, skip the first ending, and play the second ending. |

70. POLLY WOLLY DOODLE

College Song

71. CAN YOU GUESS MY NAME?

72. BAND CHORDS

Band Arrangement

73. STREETS OF LAREDO

Folk Song - Band Arrangement

74. KEY SIGNATURE QUIZ

★ Write in the note names.

THEORY GAME

W3TP

NEW IDEA

| NATURAL | ♮ | A natural sign cancels a flat or sharp. It remains in effect for the entire measure. |

75. WHO WILL PLAY ALL THE RIGHT NOTES?

76. WILL YOU GET TRICKED?

NEW IDEA

| TIME SIGNATURE | 2/4 = 2 beats in each measure | 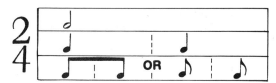 |

77. LITTLE BELLS OF WESTMINSTER
4-Part Round

★ Are you playing with a fast air stream and a good hand position?

78. THE HARPSICHORD PLAYER
Johann Sebastian Bach

★ Write in the counting before you play.

NEW IDEAS

| D.C. AL FINE | D.C. (Da Capo) = beginning Fine = finish | When you see the D.C. al Fine, go back to the beginning and stop when you come to the Fine. |
| ABA FORM | The first musical section A is followed by a new section B. Then section A is repeated. | |

79. THE STAR GAZER
Folk Melody

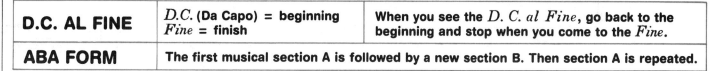

Fine   D.C. al Fine

80. CONCERTO FOR HAND CLAPPERS, KNEE SLAPPERS, and FOOT STOMPERS

SOMETHING SPECIAL...for cornets/trumpets only

W3TP

18

NEW NOTES

NEW IDEA

81. WARM-UP

1. Play on your mouthpiece only. Think "ee" and "oo."   2. Play on your instrument.

82. TONE DEVELOPER

★ Don't force the high notes. Use a faster air stream.

83. GO TELL AUNT RHODY

American Folk Song

DOTTED QUARTER NOTE

1 + ½ = 1½ beats

84. TWO WAYS TO PLAY IT

★ Write in the counting before you play.

85. QUARTERBACK SNEAK

86. AMERICA

Henry Carey

★ Are you using plenty of air?

87. FOLLOW THE LEADER

Solo/Soli   Tutti

Fine

Solo/Soli   Tutti

D. C. al Fine

W3TP

DYNAMICS	f = *forte*	Play with a full volume.
	p = *piano*	Play with a soft volume.
PICK-UP NOTES		Note or notes that come before the first full measure of a piece.

WESTERN PORTRAIT

Root/Pearson

W3TP

SPECIAL
EXERCISES

SOMETHING SPECIAL...for cornets/trumpets only

A. WARM-UP

1. Play on your instrument.   2. Play on your mouthpiece only.

B. TECHNIC TRAINER

★Always check the key signature.

C. SCALE STUDY

★Are you using good wind speed?

D. ARPEGGIO STUDY

E. THIRD STUDY

★Are you playing with a good hand position?

F. TONGUING TRAINER

★Remember...air should always follow the tongue.

G. SCALE STUDY

H. VALVE PUSHER

W3TP

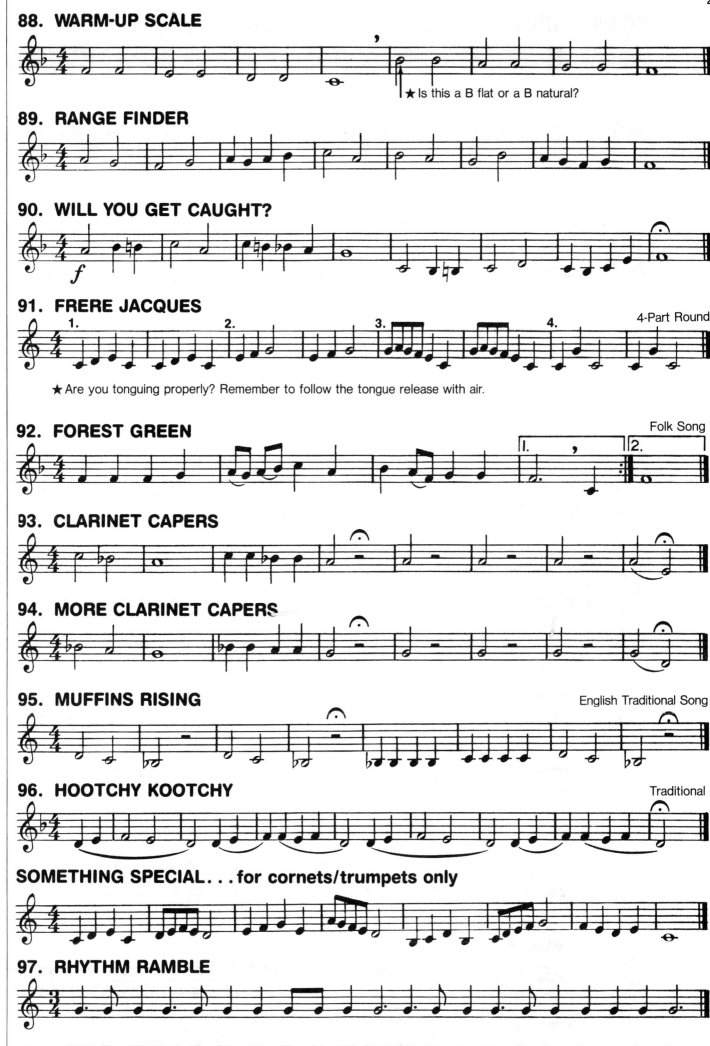

88. WARM-UP SCALE

★ Is this a B flat or a B natural?

89. RANGE FINDER

90. WILL YOU GET CAUGHT?

91. FRERE JACQUES

4-Part Round

★ Are you tonguing properly? Remember to follow the tongue release with air.

92. FOREST GREEN

Folk Song

93. CLARINET CAPERS

94. MORE CLARINET CAPERS

95. MUFFINS RISING

English Traditional Song

96. HOOTCHY KOOTCHY

Traditional

SOMETHING SPECIAL....for cornets/trumpets only

SPECIAL EXERCISE

97. RHYTHM RAMBLE

THEORY GAME

1. Draw in the bar lines.   2. Write in the counting before you play.

W3TP

22

98. WARM-UP

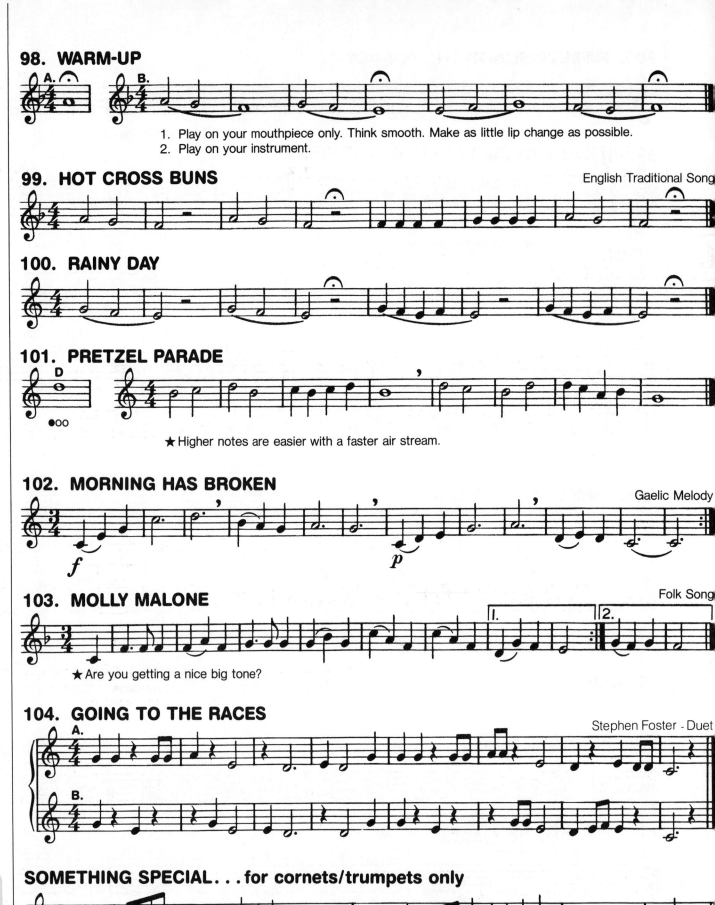

1. Play on your mouthpiece only. Think smooth. Make as little lip change as possible.
2. Play on your instrument.

99. HOT CROSS BUNS

English Traditional Song

100. RAINY DAY

101. PRETZEL PARADE

NEW NOTE

★ Higher notes are easier with a faster air stream.

102. MORNING HAS BROKEN

Gaelic Melody

103. MOLLY MALONE

Folk Song

★ Are you getting a nice big tone?

104. GOING TO THE RACES

Stephen Foster - Duet

SOMETHING SPECIAL...for cornets/trumpets only

SPECIAL
EXERCISE

105. ACCIDENTAL GAME

THEORY
GAME

1. If the second note in each measure is lower than the first note, write **L** for **lower**.
2. If it is the same as the first, write **S** for **same**.
3. If it is higher than the first, write **H** for **higher**.

W3TP

106. SWEETLY SINGS THE DONKEY

2-Part Round

107. THE DONKEY SINGS IT IN A NEW KEY

2-Part Round

TIME SIGNATURE	C = Common Time	C = 4/4

108. LONG, LONG AGO

Thomas Haynes Bayly

★ Check the key signatures.

109. FIRST DOWN MARCH

Band Arrangement

SHARP	♯		A sharp raises a note ½ step. It remains in effect for the entire measure.

110. HERITAGE SONG

Henri Hemy

111. CHROMATIC MARCH

ENHARMONIC TONES	SAME	G / F♯ / G♭ SAME	Enharmonic tones are tones that sound the same but are written differently.

112. SAME GAME

G♭ _____ B♭ _____ G♯ _____ D♯ _____

★ Write the names of enharmonic tones that match the notes.

W3TP

113. WARM-UP

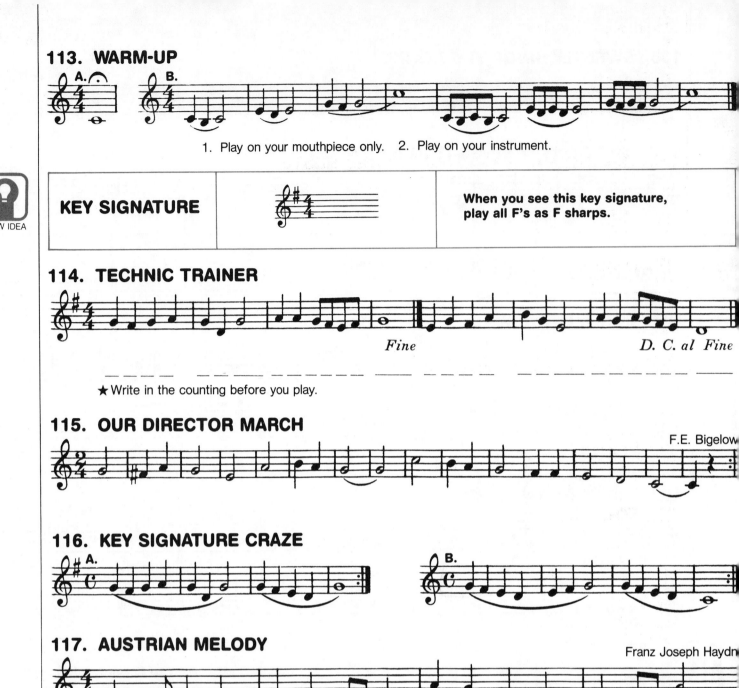

1. Play on your mouthpiece only.   2. Play on your instrument.

KEY SIGNATURE		When you see this key signature, play all F's as F sharps.

114. TECHNIC TRAINER

Fine   *D. C. al Fine*

★ Write in the counting before you play.

115. OUR DIRECTOR MARCH

F.E. Bigelow

116. KEY SIGNATURE CRAZE

117. AUSTRIAN MELODY

Franz Joseph Haydn

118. ENCORE PIECE FOR HAND CLAPPERS, KNEE SLAPPERS, and FOOT STOMPERS

Hand Clappers

Knee Slappers

Foot Stompers

SOMETHING SPECIAL...for cornets/trumpets only

SPECIAL
EXERCISE

NEW IDEA

119. SERENADE

Johann Sebastian Bach

★ Did you play the *forte* full and the *piano* soft?

120. SIMPLE GIFTS

Shaker Song

★ Are you playing with a good hand position?

121. SUNTAN SERENADE

Root - Duet

122. THIS OLD MAN HAS RHYTHM

★ Write in the counting before you play.

DIVISI	divisi (div.) = divided	Part of the section plays the top note; part plays the bottom note.

123. TIJUANA TILLY'S

Root/Pearson - Band Arrangement

★ In ¾ time a whole rest equals a whole measure (3 beats).

SOMETHING SPECIAL. . . for cornets/trumpets only

124. ACCIDENTAL GAME

1. If the second note in each measure is lower than the first note, write **L** for **lower**.
2. If it is the same as the first, write **S** for **same**.
3. If it is higher than the first, write **H** for **higher**.

W3TP

SPECIAL
EXERCISES

SOMETHING SPECIAL...for cornets/trumpets only

WARM-UP

1. Play on your instrument.   2. Play on your mouthpiece only.

C. SCALE STUDY

★ How's your wind speed?

D. TECHNIC TRAINER

★ Is your hand position correct?

E. GETTING THERE

★ Be sure you don't force the high notes!

F. DO THE DIATONIC

G. TONGUING TRAINER

★ Use plenty of air!

W3TP

125. A CHROMATIC VIEW POINT

126. ACCIDENTAL ANTICS

★ Remember the key signature.

127. CROSSING THAT BREAK

★ Use plenty of air!

128. CHROMATIC MARCH RE-VISITED

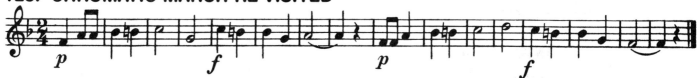

NEW IDEA

AABA FORM	The first musical section A is played two times, followed by a new section B. Then section A is repeated.

129. ALL THROUGH THE NIGHT

Old Welsh Song - Band Arrangement

★ Listen for each section of the form.

130. SEE, THE CONQUERING HERO COMES

George Frideric Handel

131. FOLLOW THE LEADER

THEORY
GAME

132. NAME GAME

★ Write in the note names and their accidentals.

W3TP

DYNAMICS	 = *crescendo* (cresc.) = *decrescendo* (decresc.)	**Gradually play louder.** **Gradually play softer.**

133. WARM-UP

134. BOOGIE BEAT

Root - Duet

135. CHROMATIC WALTZ

136. THE MINSTREL BOY

Folk Song

THEME AND VARIATIONS	A simple tune followed by the same tune with changes.

137. WHERE DID MY LITTLE DOG GO?

German Song

Theme

Variation

SOMETHING SPECIAL. . .for cornets/trumpets only

W3TP

EW IDEA

| DYNAMICS | *mp* = *mezzo piano* | Play with a medium soft volume. |
| | *mf* = *mezzo forte* | Play with a medium full volume. |

138. SCARBOROUGH FAIR

English Folk Song

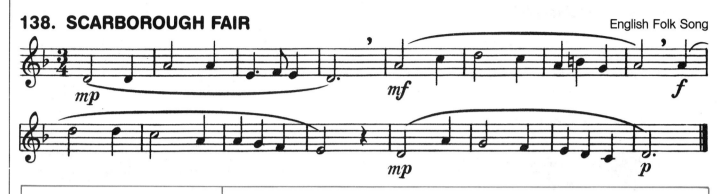

NEW IDEA

| PHRASE | A musical thought or sentence. The end of a phrase is a good place to take a breath. |

139. POLISHED PHRASES

Root - Band Arrangement

NEW IDEA

TEMPOS	Andante = moderately slow
	Moderato = moderate speed
	Allegro = quick and lively

140. BRING A TORCH

French Song

Moderato

★Check your hand position.

141. BAYSIDE BOUNCE

Root/Pearson -Band Arrangement

Allegro

142. CHROMATIC CAPER

Andante

143. PUTTING IT ALL TOGETHER

★Are you using a steady air stream?

W3TP

144. HONEY ROCK FLAPJACKS

Band Arrangement

145. FROGGIE'S WALTZ

Root/Pearson - Trio

Spoken: "Rib-bit"

146. EARLY AMERICAN SALUTE

Billings/Pearson - Duet

147. JINGLE BELLS

Pierpont/Pearson - Band Arrangement

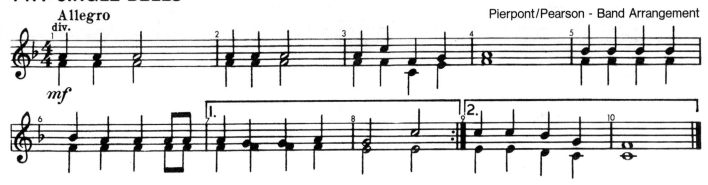

148. COWBOYS AND CACTUS

Root/Pearson - Band Arrangement

149. BUMPY ROAD

Band Arrangement